Getting Ready to Write

A B C D
a b c d

The Lion and the Mouse

1. Pretend you are the mouse.
   Tell the story about you and the lion.

2. Pretend you are the lion.
   Tell the story about you and the mouse.

3. Tell about something kind you have done for someone.
   How did you feel about doing it?

3

a　　*b*　　*c*　　*d*

e　　*f*　　*g*　　*h*

i　　*j*　　*k*　　*l*

m　　*n*　　*o*　　*p*

q　　*r*　　*s*　　*t*

u　　*v*　　*w*　　*x*

y　　*z*

The Capital Letters

A   B   C   D

E   F   G   H

I   J   K   L

M   N   O   P

Q   R   S   T

U   V   W   X

Y   Z

Sit tall.
Keep both feet
on the floor.

Slant your paper like this.
Hold it steady with your right hand.

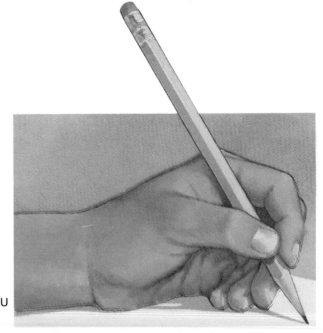

Look at the picture.
Then look at how you
hold your pencil.

Right-handed Writers

Slant your paper like this.
Hold it steady with your left hand.

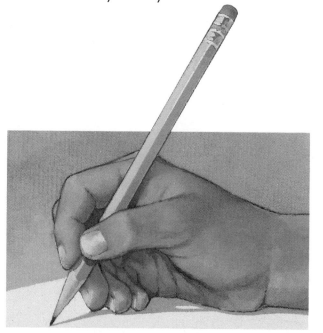

Sit tall.
Keep both feet
on the floor.

Look at the picture.
Then look at how you
hold your pencil.

Top, Middle, and Bottom

Circle.

Teacher's Directions: Tell students to circle the top bear, the middle pig, and the bottom goat.

Top to Bottom

Draw a line.

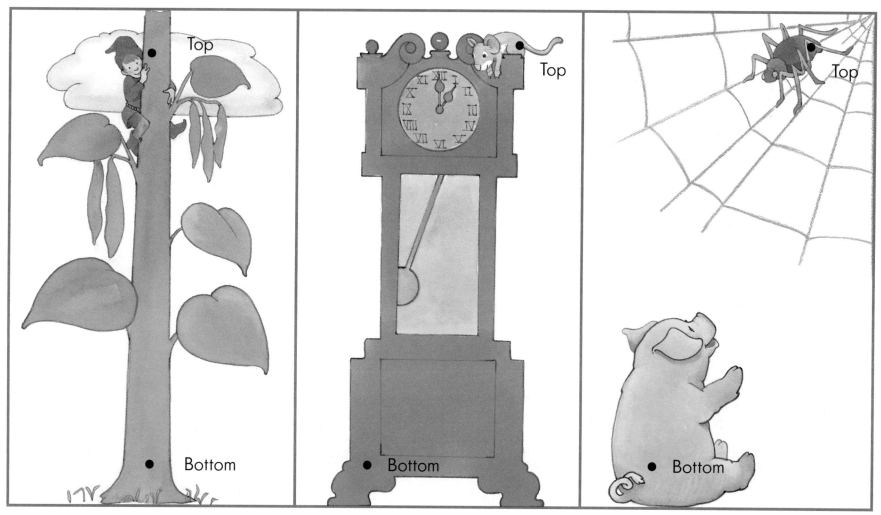

Top

Bottom

Top

Bottom

Top

Bottom

Teacher's Directions: Have students help each storybook character get down by drawing a line from the dot near the word *top* to the dot near the word *bottom*.

Circle.

Teacher's Directions: For each pair of objects, direct students to circle the object on the left or to circle the object on the right.

Left to Right

Draw a line.

Left

Right

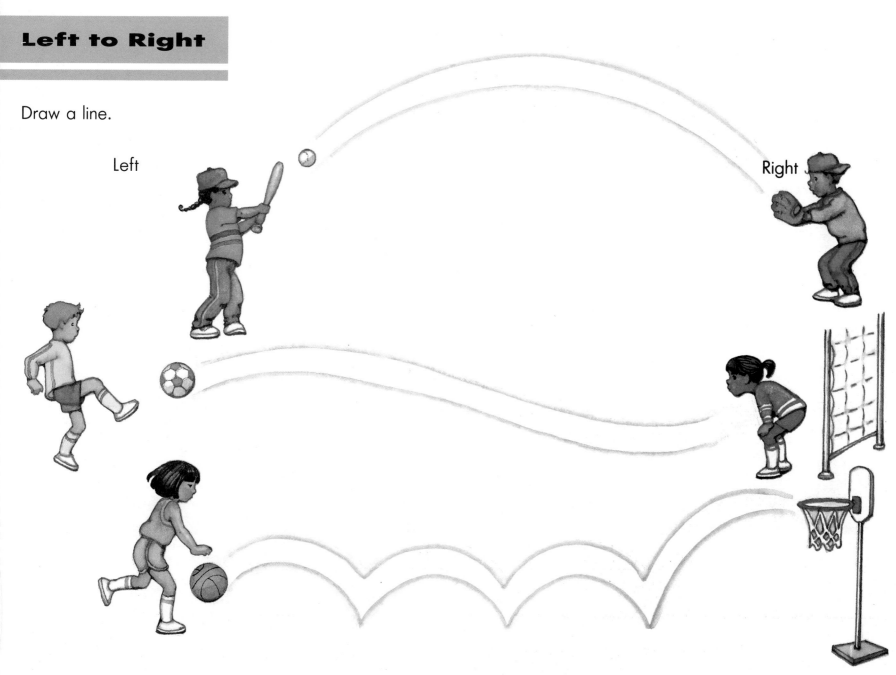

Teacher's Directions: Tell students to draw a line from left to right along each path.

11

Circle the picture or letter that matches the one in the box.

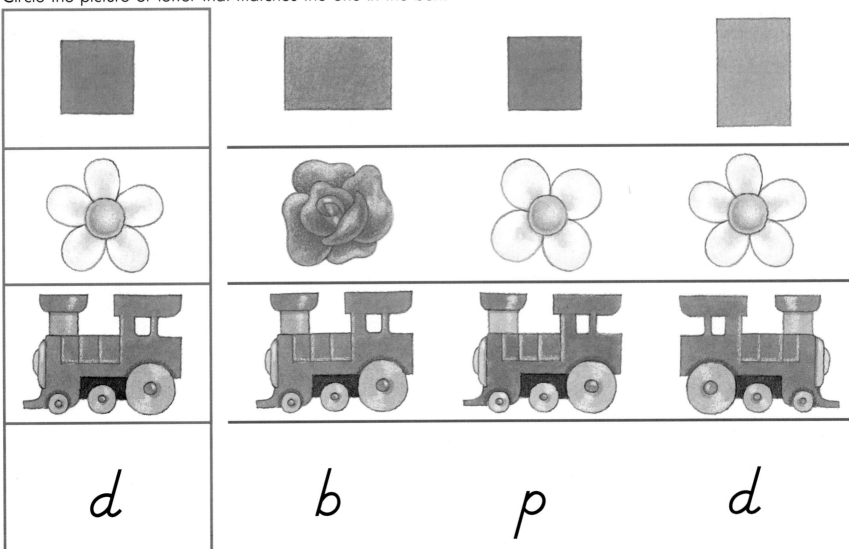

Which Ones Are Alike?

Circle the letter that matches the one in the box.

c	e c o

S	X S Z

T	L F T

h	k h n

m	m n w

G	Q C G

B	E R B

g	g q y

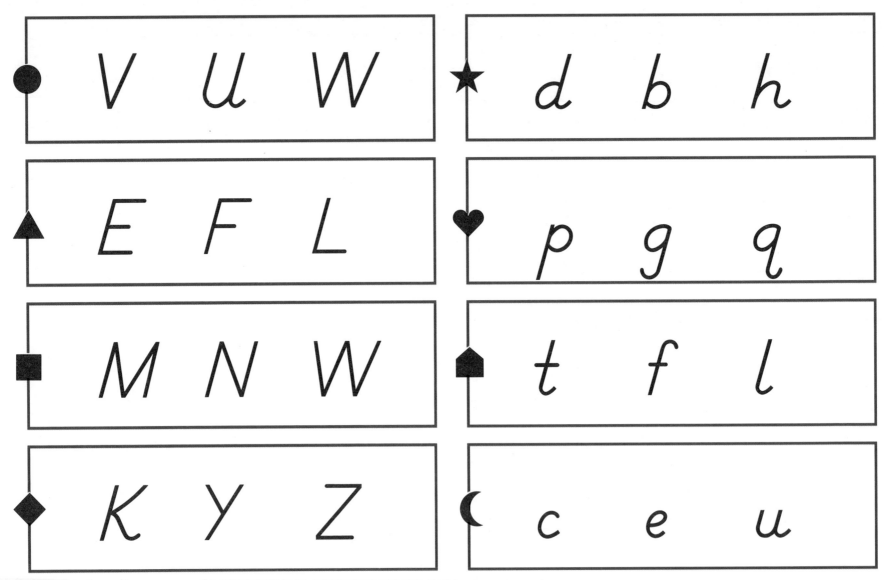

Teacher's Directions: Have students circle the following letters: **V, F, N, Z, b, q, t, e.**

Letter Slant

Some things are straight.

Some things slant.

In handwriting, letters slant.
All your letters should slant the same way.

My robot helps me.

Circle the letters that slant.

d   i   t   m   L   B   C   F   A

Here are the shapes you will need to write letters.
In handwriting, these shapes are called **strokes.**

Look at the colored strokes in the letters below.

Trace these letters.

N   m   f   Q   k   d

Trace and write each stroke.

Letter Size

dog

Letters come in different sizes.

Some reach high.

These letters touch the top line and the baseline.

l t k d h b f

Some sit low.

These letters touch the midline and the baseline.

i o a c e s n m

r u w v x z

Some go below.

These letters touch the midline and the descender line.

g p y q j

18

Reach High	Sit Low	Go Below

l   t   k

d   h   b

f

i   o   a   c   e

s   n   m   r   u

w   v   x   z

g   g   p   y

q   j

Circle the letters that reach high.

j   e   f

v   k   q

m   b   d

Circle the letters that sit low.

r   g   t

w   n   y

z   h   c

Circle the letters that go below.

y   k   q

r   p   a

d   e   g

Letter and Word Spacing

Leave the space of a pencil point between letters.

Correct

just right

Incorrect

too close

too far

Leave the space of a pencil between words.

Correct

like this

Incorrect

not like this

Smoothness

Good handwriting is smooth.
The lines are even and flowing.

Tell which handwriting is best.

too light   shaky

too dark   **too thick**

just right

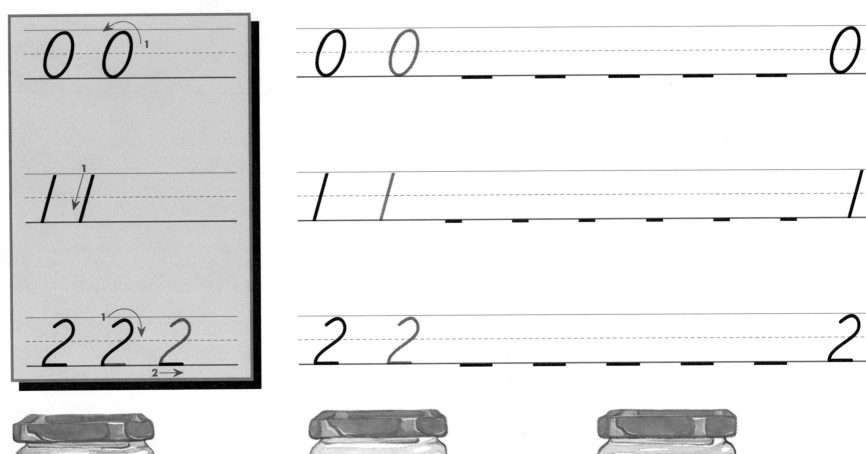

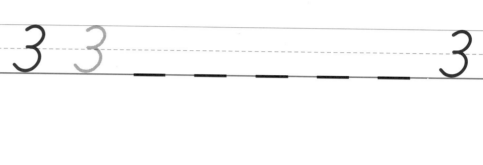

3 3 3

4 4 4

5 5 5

3

4

5

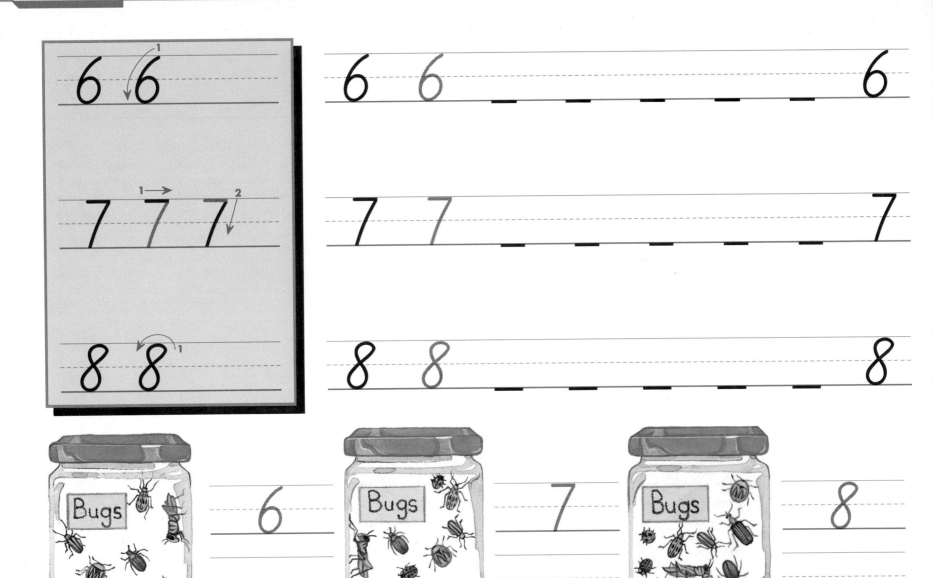

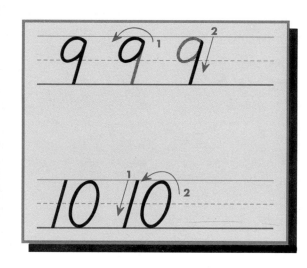

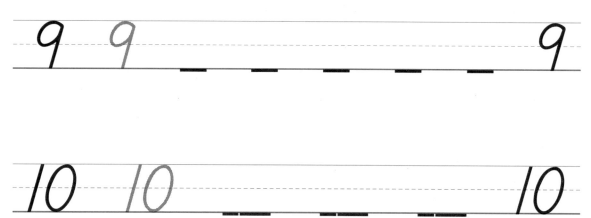

9   9   9

10   10   10

   9

   10

25

Circle the words that slant correctly.

bat   ball   mitt   cap

Circle the letters that reach high.
Underline the letters that go below.

s   h   j   o   y   l

Circle the words that show correct spacing.

good w or k   good work

UNIT 2

Writing Just for Me

For School
pencil
paper
book

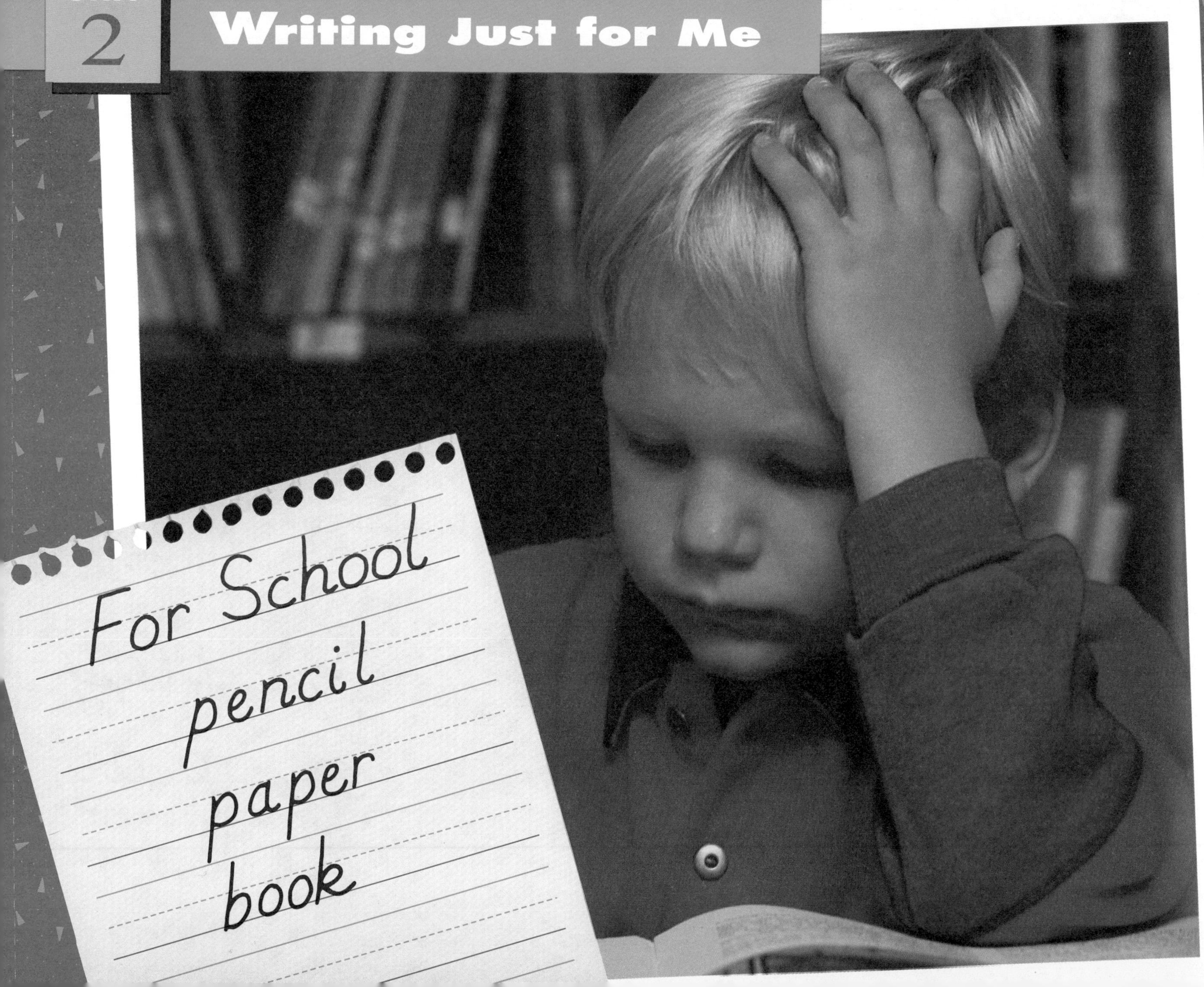

l

l l l l l l l

l l l

l l l

learn   help   play

_earn   he_p   p_ay

28   **SELF CHECK**   Circle your best l .

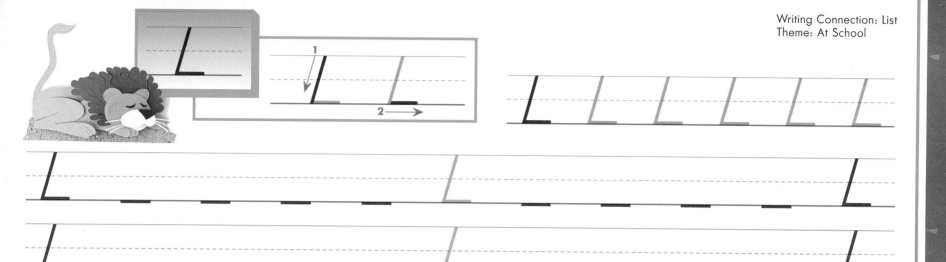

Look at us learn.

_ook at us _earn.

⭐ **SPEAKING AND LISTENING** Tell something you have learned at school this year.

i

$\downarrow$ *i* *i*

i i i i i i

i   *i*   *i*

i   *i*   *i*

paint

pa_nt

scissors

sc_ssors

  SELF CHECK   Circle your best *i* .

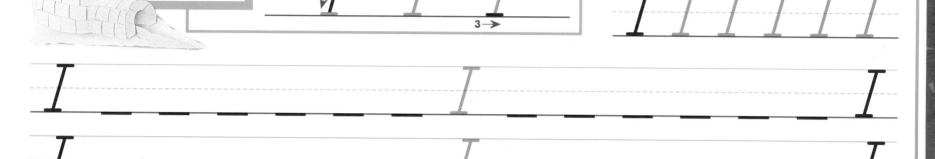

I paint rainbows.

_pa_nt ra_nbows.

SPEAKING AND LISTENING   Tell what you like to draw or paint.

31

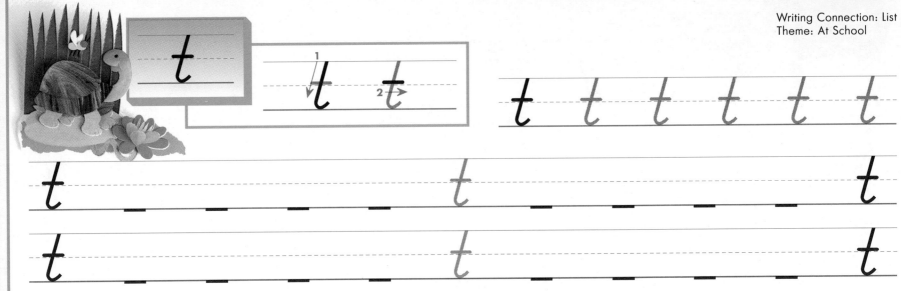

_t_   _t_   _t_   _t_   _t_   _t_   _t_

_t_   _t_   _t_

_t_   _t_   _t_

tell stories

_e _ _ s or _ es_

count

_coun _

SELF CHECK   Circle a _t_ that touches the top line and the baseline.

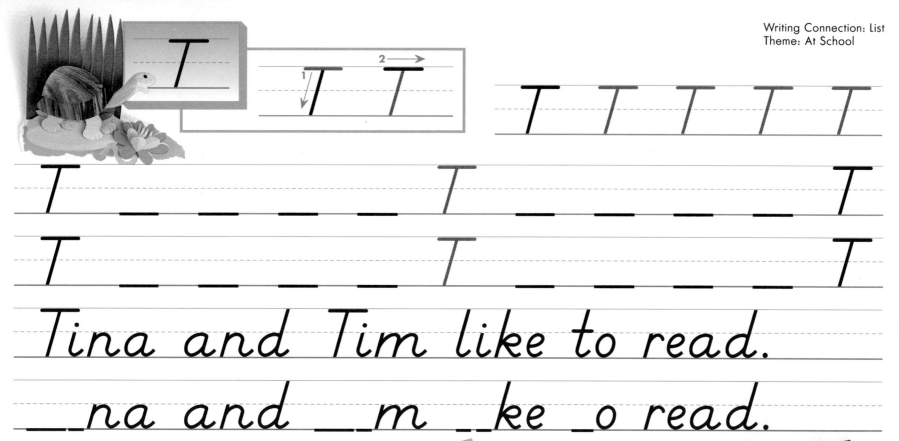

T T T T T

T _ _ _ _ T _ _ _ _ T

T _ _ _ _ T _ _ _ _ T

Tina and Tim like to read.

__na and __m __ke _o read.

★ **SPEAKING AND LISTENING** Tell what you like to do at school.

33

Writing a List

Make a list of your school friends.

School Friends

34  **ON YOUR OWN** Make a list of people in your family.

Write the letters and words.

L   L   l   I   i   T   t

it   lit   ill

Circle the letter you wrote best.

Circle the word you wrote best.

O

O

O   O   O   O   O   O

O   O   O

O   O   O

books
b__ks

toys
__ys

tools
___s

SPEAKING AND LISTENING Tell about a sign you have made.

O   O   O   O   O   O

O   O   O

O   O   O

Olga   Olivia   Oscar

___ga   ___v a   ___scar

 **ASK A FRIEND**   Have a friend circle your best O.

a

$\overset{\curvearrowleft}{a}{}^1$ $\overset{2}{a}$

a a a a a a

a _ _ _ _ _ _ _ a _ _ _ _ _ _ a

a _ _ _ _ _ _ _ a _ _ _ _ _ _ a

alligator

_ _ _ g _ _ r

seal   bear

se _ _   be _ r

SELF CHECK   Circle your best a .

A A A A A

A _____ A _____ A

A _____ A _____ A

Alligators are amazing.

___g___rs ___re ___m_z_ng.

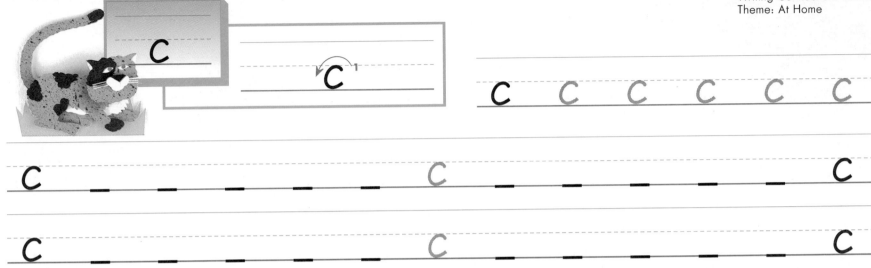

c

c c c c c c

c _ _ _ _ c _ _ _ _ _ _ c

c _ _ _ _ c _ _ _ _ _ c

carrots

_ _ rr _ _ s

corn

_ _ rn

lettuce

_ e _ _ u _ e

★ ON YOUR OWN   Make a list of vegetables you like to eat.

C

C   C   C   C   C   C

C   C   C

C   C   C

Carol plants a garden.

__ r __ p __ n s __ g __ rden.

ASK A FRIEND   Have a friend circle your best C and tell why it is best.

Writing Labels

Write the missing letters.

At the Ocean

__ he __e__n

Our Family

__ur F__m__y

42  **ON YOUR OWN**   Draw a picture of your family. Label your drawing.

Write what the wee little bear might say about his day.

Evaluation

Write the letters and words.

O o A a C c

cat cool tall

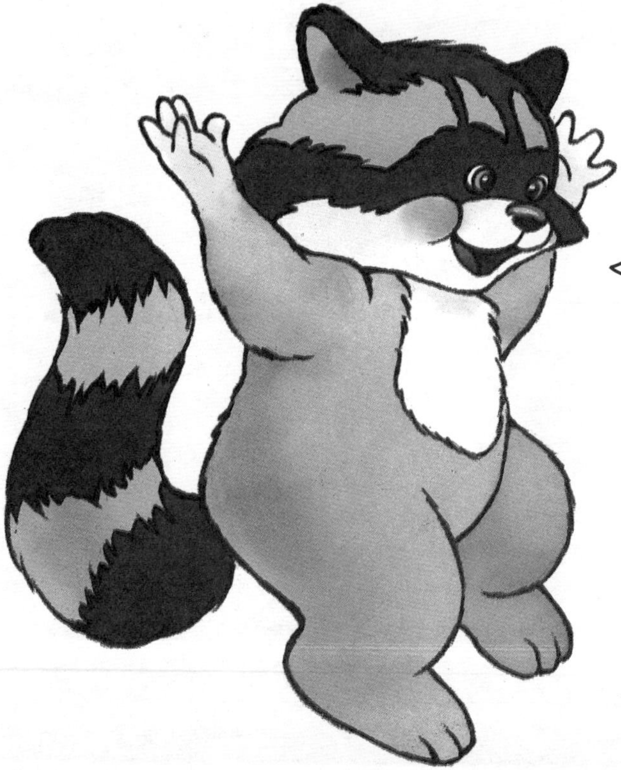
Circle the letter you wrote best.

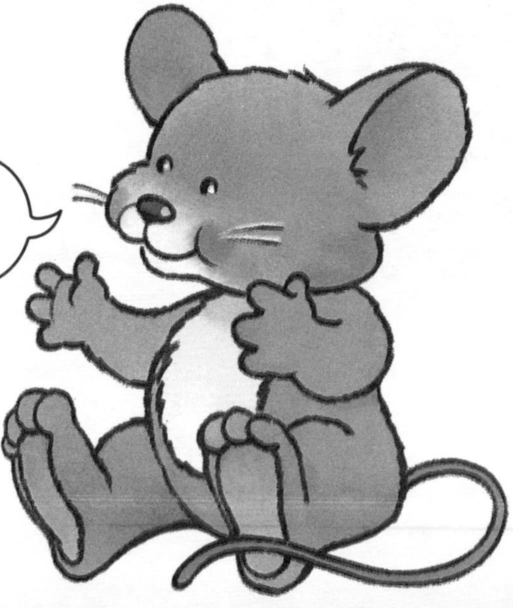
Circle the word you wrote best.

Zoo	Pets
lion	kitten
seal	fish

d   d   d   d   d   d   d   d   d   d

d _ _ _ _ _ _ _ _ _ _ _ _ d _ _ _ _ _ _ _ _ _ _ _ d

d _ _ _ _ _ _ _ _ _ _ _ _ d _ _ _ _ _ _ _ _ _ _ _ d

duckling duck

_u_k_ _ng _ _u_k

tadpole toad

_ _ _p_e _ _ _ _

46  **SELF CHECK**   Circle your best *d* .

D D D

D D D D D D

D   D   D

D   D   D

Do ducklings dive?

__ __ u k __ ngs __ ve?

SPEAKING AND LISTENING   Tell what you would like to learn about ducklings.

g g g²

g g g g g g

g _ _ _ _ _ _ _ _ _ g _ _ _ _ _ _ _ g

g _ _ _ _ _ _ _ _ _ g _ _ _ _ _ _ _ g

egg   gosling   goose

e__   __ s __ n __   __ __ se

 **ASK A FRIEND**   Have a friend circle your best *g* .

48

G

G¹ G²

G G G G G G

G   G   G

G   G   G

Goslings eat grain.

__ s __ ngs e __ __ r __ n.

★ **SPEAKING AND LISTENING**   Share another fact about baby birds.

Linking Handwriting to Writing

Making a Chart

Trace each word. Then write the word.

Animal Babies	Adults
puppy	dog ___
kid	goat ___
piglet	pig p__

 **ON YOUR OWN**   Make your own chart of animal babies and adults.

Trace each word. Then write the word.

dog

goat

toad

Gil

Dot

Gail

Circle a word in which all the letters slant the same way.

Circle the word you wrote best.

e

e   e   e   e   e   e

e _ _ _ _ _ _ _ _ *e* _ _ _ _ _ _ _ _ *e*

e _ _ _ _ _ _ _ _ *e* _ _ _ _ _ _ _ _ *e*

elephant

*__ph_n_*

giraffe

*__r_ff_*

52  **SELF CHECK**   Circle your best *e*.

E

E E E

E E E E E

E   E   E

E   E   E

Every elephant can swim.

v_ry __ph_n_ __n sw_m.

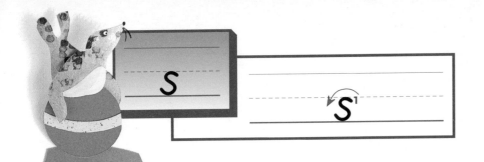

s

s¹

s s s s s s

s   s   s

s   s   s

snakes _n_k_

lizards _z_r_

ASK A FRIEND   Ask a friend to circle your best s .

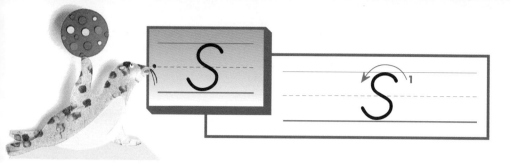

S

S S S S S S

S   S   S

S   S   S

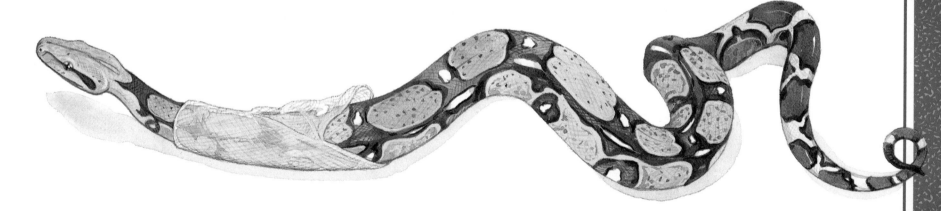

Snakes shed their skins.
_n_k_ _h_ _h_r_k_n_.

 **SPEAKING AND LISTENING** Tell something you know about snakes or other reptiles.

Linking Handwriting to Writing

Labeling a Map

Take a trip through this zoo. Write the letters and words along the path.

ZOO

bears

b _ _ r _

seals

elephants

_ _ _ ph _ n _

56

tigers

__ __r__

camels

__ __m__ __

crocodiles

__r__ __ __ __ __ __

ON YOUR OWN   Be a zoo planner. Make a map of your new zoo.

57

n

n n n n n n n n

n ___ ___ ___ ___ n ___ ___ ___ n

n ___ ___ ___ ___ n ___ ___ ___ n

ponies   kittens

p___ ___ ___   k___ ___ ___

⭐ **SPEAKING AND LISTENING**   Tell a friend about your favorite animal.

N

N N N N

N N N N

N   N   N

N   N   N

Neil wants a kitten.

___ w ___ k ___.

No one else does.

_____.

SELF CHECK Circle the N you wrote that has the best slant.

m

m *m* *m*

m m m m

m _ _ _ _ _ _ _ _ *m* _ _ _ _ _ _ _ *m*

m _ _ _ _ _ _ _ _ *m* _ _ _ _ _ _ _ *m*

monkey

_ _ _ k_y

el mono

_ _ _ _ _

 **ASK A FRIEND**   Ask a friend to circle your best *m* and underline an *m* that needs work.

M

1 ↓ M 2 ↓ M 3 ↗ M 4 ↓ M

M M M

M   M   M

M   M   M

Mia likes monkeys.

_____ k _____ k _ y .

Miguel likes lambs.

_____ u _ k _____ b .

Linking Handwriting to Writing

Making a Picture Graph

Trace each word. Then write the word.

Our Favorite Animals

lions

mice

moose

  **ON YOUR OWN** Invite your family and friends to name a favorite animal.

The Enormous Turnip

Think of another way the farmer might get the turnip out of the ground. Draw a picture to show your idea. Write a sentence to tell about your picture.

Trace each word. Then write the word.

ants

snails

camels

Nina

Matt

Naomi

Circle the word you wrote best.

Circle a word in which all the letters slant the same way.

I have a fluffy white dog.

h

h   h

_h_   _h_   _h_   _h_   _h_

_h_ _h_ _ _ _ _ _ _ _ _ _ _ _ _ _ _ _h_

_h_ _h_ _ _ _ _ _ _ _ _ _ _ _ _ _ _ _h_

hot

_h_

hotter

_ _ _ _ _r

hottest

SELF CHECK   Circle your best _h_ .

H

H H H H H H

H   H   H

H   H

Heidi swings high.

_____ w _____ ___.

Hoshi swings higher.

_____ w _____ __ r.

higher

high

ON YOUR OWN Draw pictures to explain the words *light, lighter, lightest.*

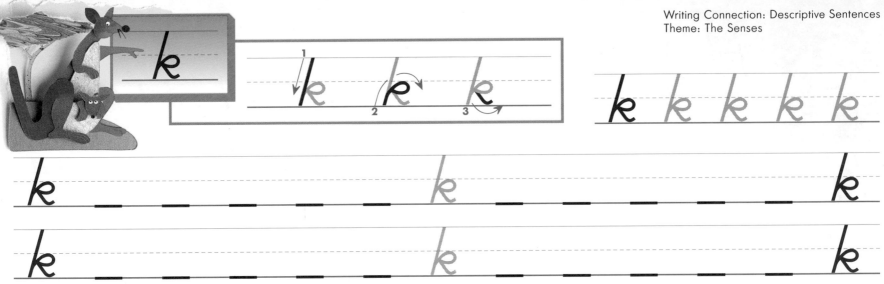

k *k* *k* *k* *k*

k *k* *k*

k *k* *k*

Trace and write each sound word. Tell what sound goes with each picture.

tick *honk* *click*

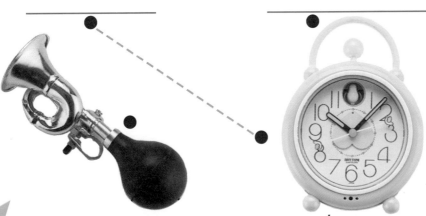

⭐ **ASK A FRIEND** Ask a friend to circle your best *k* and underline a *k* that could be better.

K

K K K

K K K K K

K _ _ _ _ _ _ K _ _ _ _ _ K

K _ _ _ _ _ _ K _ _ _ K

Kettles whistle.

_ _ _ _ _ _ w _ _ _ _ .

Keys jingle.

_ _ y _ j _ _ _ _ .

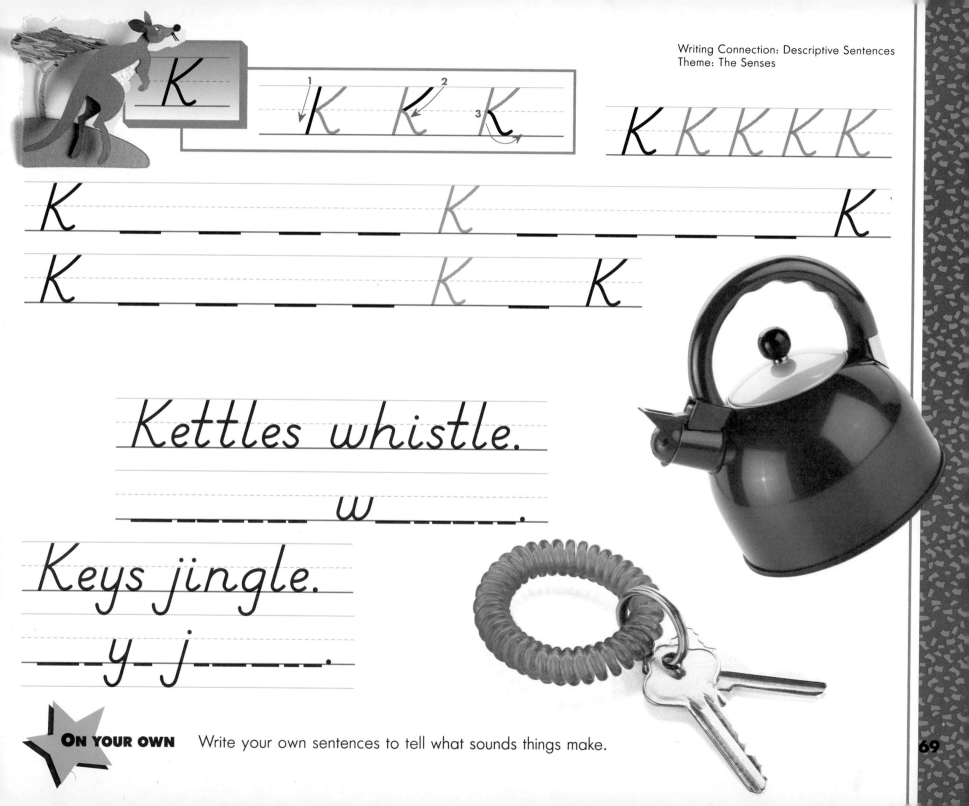

ON YOUR OWN   Write your own sentences to tell what sounds things make.

69

Using Punctuation — The Period

A sentence that tells something is a **statement.**
Use a period at the end of a statement.

Trace and write each sentence.

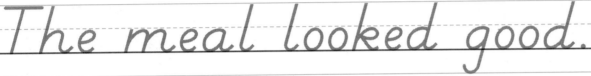

The meal looked good.

Hank smelled the onions.

The chili tasted hot.

  **ON YOUR OWN**   Write a statement about your favorite food.

Using Punctuation

The Question Mark

A sentence that asks something is a **question.**
A question ends with a question mark.

Trace and write a row of question marks.
Then write each question.

? ? ? ?   ?

Can meat sizzle?

_____ zz___

Do peaches feel smooth?

__ p____ f_____

 **ON YOUR OWN**   Write a question about a food.

Writing Descriptive Sentences

Proofreading Proofreading means looking for mistakes in your writing.

Here are two proofreading marks you can use to correct mistakes.

Proofreading Marks
☰ Use a capital letter. <u>h</u>anna
⊙ Add a period. See me⊙

Tell why each proofreading mark was needed.

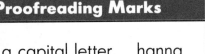

the moon is shining.

The lake looks like glass.

⌨ **COMPUTER TIP** Press the shift key and then a letter key to make a capital letter on a computer.

Use proofreading marks to correct errors in capital letters and periods.

the old tent leaked

I got soaked

Final Draft Write each sentence. Make the corrections that your proofreading marks show.

HANDWRITING TIP Remember to space your words evenly.

ON YOUR OWN Write a sentence or two to describe a rainstorm.

73

b

b   b   b   b

b   b   b

b   b   b

top   above

__p_   ___v_

bottom   below

                                                      ___w

 **ON YOUR OWN**   Make a list of other word pairs that are opposites.

B

B B B B

B B B B

B B B

B B B

Buses are big.

_u___ r____.

Bikes are small.

____ r____.

SELF CHECK   Circle a *B* that has top and bottom loops the same size.

75

p

p   p   p   p   p   p   p

p   p   p

p   p   p

stop   go

push   pull

u   u

PPPP

STOP

ASK A FRIEND Ask a friend to circle your best p.

P

P   P   P   P   P   P

P   P   P

P   P

P   P

Pablo is happy.

_____ y.

Pat is sad.

ON YOUR OWN   Write some sentence pairs that use opposites to describe two houses.

Making an Opposites Chart

Trace and write the words.

Opposites

big

little

open

closed

 **ON YOUR OWN**   Create your own opposites chart using words and pictures.

78

Write each sentence.

Pam plants beans.

Bill picks them.

Circle the capital letter you wrote best.

Circle the word you wrote best.

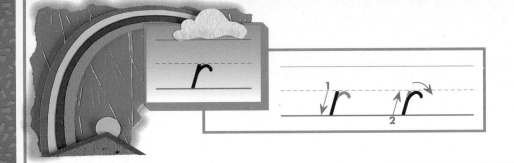

r   r   r   r   r   r   r   r

r — — — — — — r — — — — — — — r

r — — — — — — r — — — — — — — r

red   *rojo*

j — — —

green   *verde*

v — — —

80    **SELF CHECK**   Circle your best *r* .

R

R R R

R R R R

R

R

R

R

R

R

Rosa has a red

and green parrot.

ON YOUR OWN

Write another sentence that tells more about Rosa's parrot.

f f f f f f f

f — — — — — f

f — — — — — f

furry bears

_u__y_____

furry brown bears

_u__y___w_____

 **ASK A FRIEND**   Have a friend circle one of your *f*'s that is crossed at the midline.

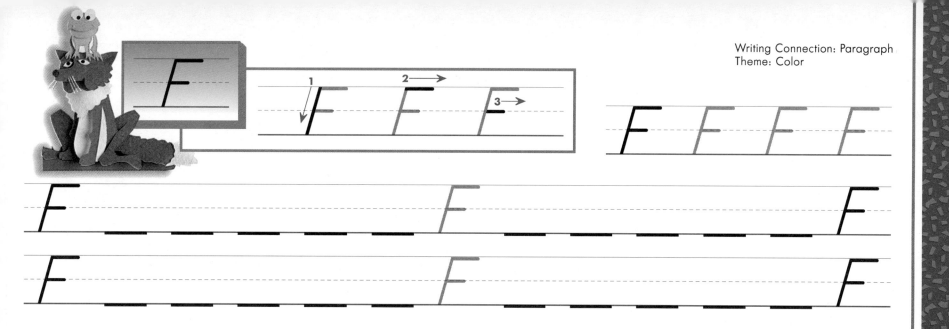

F F F F

F   F   F

F   F   F

Four furry brown bears
looked for honey.

   u   u   y   w

y.

ON YOUR OWN   Write another sentence that tells what one of the bears did.

Linking Handwriting to Writing

Writing a Paragraph

A **paragraph** is a group of sentences.
All the sentences tell about one idea.
The first sentence is always indented.

Read Teresa's paragraph.

Fred sits beside me.
He has red hair and
freckles. One of his
front teeth is missing.
I like Fred.

On a computer keyboard there is a key that indents for you.

🖳 **COMPUTER TIP** Find this key on your computer.

Write Teresa's paragraph.
Remember to indent
the first word.

ON YOUR OWN   Write a paragraph that describes the person beside you.

u

¹↓u   u²↓

u   u   u   u   u   u

u _ _ _ _ _   u _ _ _ _ _   u

u _ _ _ _ _   u _ _ _ _ _   u

Trace and write the words. Then tell what animal answers the riddle.

smooth fur

soft purr

What am I?

 ON YOUR OWN   Write a riddle for another animal on this page.

U U

U U U U U U U

U U U

U U U

Under the house
I caught a mouse.

 **SELF CHECK** Circle your best U.

87

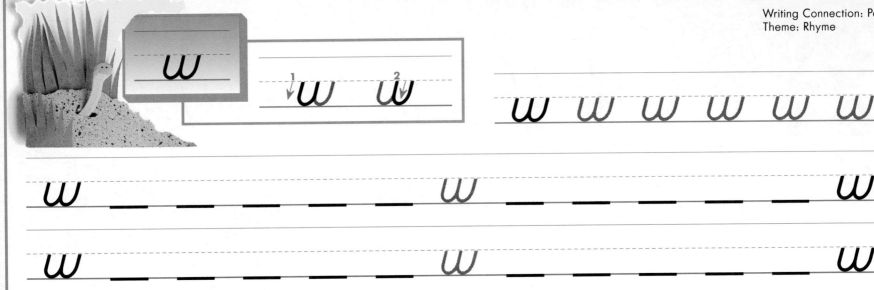

w w w w w w w w

w   w   w

w   w   w

Trace and write the words. Draw a picture to answer the riddle.

small paws

long claws

What am I?

 **ON YOUR OWN**   Make a list of words that describe different kinds of cats.

W W W W W

1 2 3 4

W W

W W W

W W W

Where will I nap?
Warm, in your lap.

 **ASK A FRIEND** Ask a friend to circle your best W.

Writing a Poem

Write this poem by Annette Wynne.

The House Cat

The house cat sits
And smiles and sings.
He knows a lot
Of secret things.

ON YOUR OWN   Write your own poem that describes how something or someone moves.

The old man was especially fond of pancakes. What is your favorite food? Make a list of words that tell how it smells and tastes.

Write the paragraph.

Wags is our dog. He is brown. Wags runs fast.

Circle the letter you wrote best.

Circle a word in which all the letters are shaped correctly.

92

The
Little
Spider

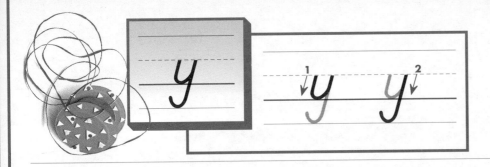

y   y   y²

y   y   y   y   y   y   y

y   y   y

y   y   y

Many years ago there was a young mouse.

ON YOUR OWN

Write the sentence again. Change the underlined word to a person or animal you would like to write about.

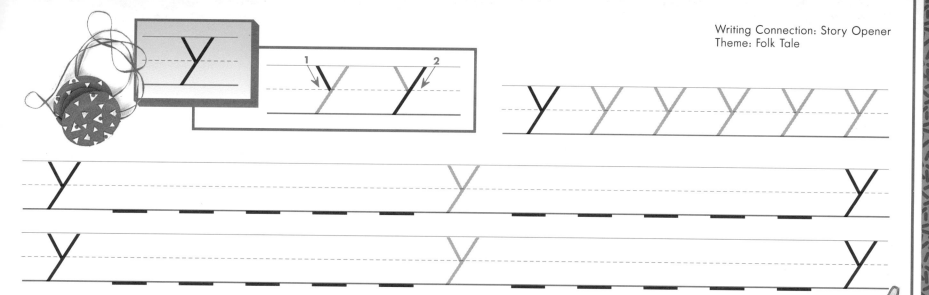

Y   Y Y Y Y Y Y

Y   Y

Y   Y

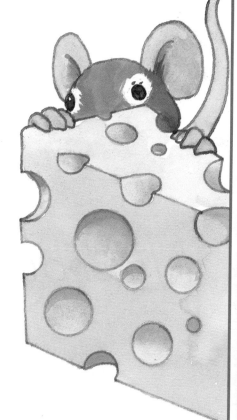

His name was Yuri the
Younger. Yuri was shy.

ON YOUR OWN   Write the sentence again. Change the underlined word to
another word that could describe a person or an animal.

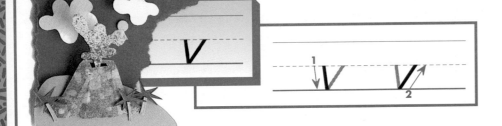

V

V   V   V   V   V   V   V   V   V   V

V   V   V

V   V   V

Nearby lived five <u>*cats*</u>*.*

 ON YOUR OWN

Write the sentence again. Change the underlined word to something else that might live nearby.

V V V V V V V V

V   V   V

V   V   V

Very soon there
was trouble.

SELF CHECK   Circle the word with the best spacing between letters.

Linking Handwriting to Writing

Writing a Story Opener

Proofreading Use proofreading marks to correct mistakes in capital letters and periods.

Proofreading Marks
≡ Use a capital letter.   <u>h</u>e was a mouse.
⊙ Add a period.   The cats were near⊙

Many years ago there was a young mouse His name was Yuri the Younger. yuri was shy. Nearby lived five cats very soon there was trouble.

💻 **COMPUTER TIP** Find the period key on your computer keyboard. Type a row of periods.

Final Draft   Write a final draft of this story opener.
Make the corrections that your proofreading marks show.

HANDWRITING TIP   Remember to leave a pencil space
between words. Leave a finger space
between sentences.

ON YOUR OWN   What do you think the trouble was? Write what happened next.

99

X   X   X   X   X   X   X

X   X   X

X   X   X

Max mixed the dough.

  **ON YOUR OWN** Tell about a time you worked with someone to prepare a special meal.

X X X X X X

X X X

X X X

Xavier fixed the toppings.

 **SELF CHECK** Circle the word with the best spacing between letters.

Z

Z   Z   Z

Z   Z   Z   Z   Z

Z   Z   Z

Z   Z   Z

Liza made pizza sauce.

ASK A FRIEND   Have a friend circle the word with the best spacing between letters.

Z

1→   2   3→

Z Z Z

Z Z Z Z

Z   Z   Z

Z   Z   Z

Zara dropped the pizza.

⭐ **ON YOUR OWN**   Make a list of toppings you would put on a pizza.

Linking Handwriting to Writing

Writing a Pattern Story

Copy the story on your paper.

Max mixed the dough.

Xavier fixed the toppings.

Liza made pizza sauce.

Zara dropped the pizza.

What happened next?

  **ON YOUR OWN** Add another line to the story to tell what happened next.

Write these sentences.

Alex fixed a tasty stew.

Zelda took it to the zoo.

Circle the word you wrote best.

Circle a word that has all the letters spaced correctly.

105

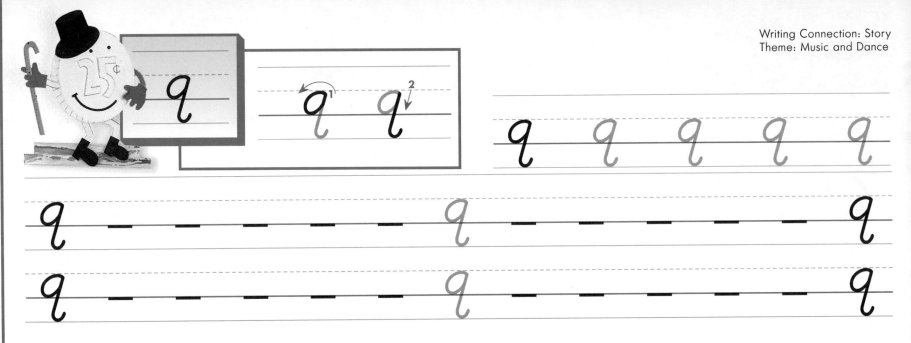

q

q^1 q^2

q q q q q

q q q

q q q

The night was quiet.
It was not quite eight.

  **ASK A FRIEND**   Invite a friend to circle any *q*'s that do not touch the descender line.

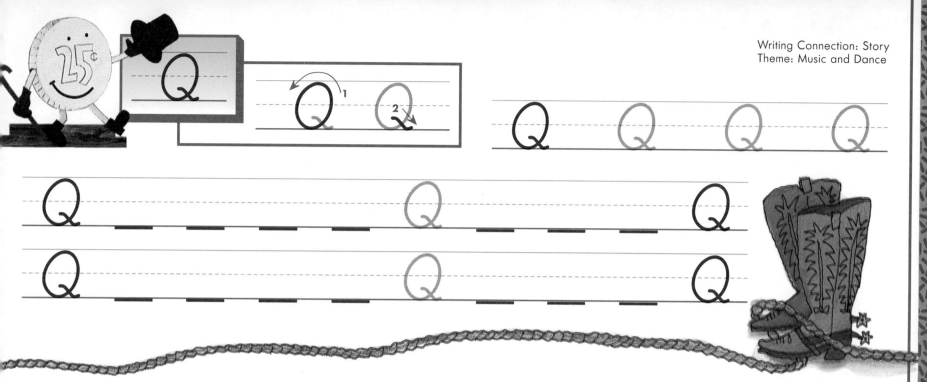

Q Q Q Q

Q Q Q

Q Q Q

Quickly Quinn headed for the square dance.

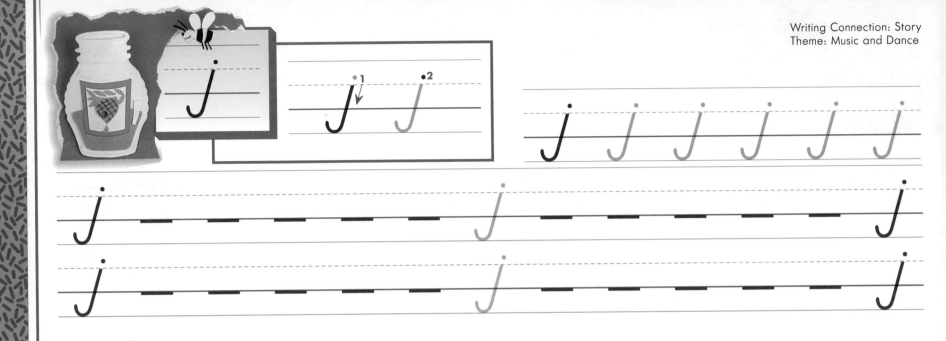

j j j j j j j

j   j   j

j   j   j

The jamboree had started.

Quinn joined in the fun.

  **SELF CHECK**   Circle a place where the spacing between words could be better.

J *J*

J   *J*   *J*   *J*   *J*   *J*   *J*   *J*

J   *J*   *J*

J   *J*   *J*

Jenny played her banjo.

Joey danced a jig.

 **ON YOUR OWN**   Write how you think the story might end.

109

Linking Handwriting to Writing

Writing a Story

Read the story.

The Jumping Jamboree

The night was quiet. It was not quite eight.
Quickly Quinn headed for the square dance.

The jamboree had started. Quinn joined in the fun.
Jenny played her banjo. Joey danced a jig.

Just then a bell rang.
Quinn sat up in bed. He
was wearing his pajamas.
It had all been just
a dream.

COMPUTER TIP Remember that to leave space between words on a computer, you must press the space bar once.

Copy the story ending.

_____

- -

_____

- -

_____

- -

_____

- -

_____

- -

_____

ON YOUR OWN   Jot down ideas for a story you would like to write. Choose one of the ideas
and write your own story.

Some handwriting is hard to read. Here are some reasons why.

Curved strokes are too straight.

Letters are not closed

Miles made an eayle.

Loops are added.

Tell what makes this handwriting hard to read.

Nadiu made a lion.

112

Pretend you are Little Red Hen. Tell how you would get the animals to help you.

Write these sentences.

Quincy jumped for joy.

Jan liked the quilt.

Circle a word that has all the letters spaced correctly.

Circle the word you wrote best.

114

Happy
Birthday
to You

Linking Handwriting to Writing

Writing an Invitation

Read the invitation below. What facts does it tell you?

For

Kim Lee

When

Saturday

July 18, noon

Where

239 Oak Street

Fill in this invitation. Use the facts from page 116.

For

When

Where

ON YOUR OWN Write an invitation of your own.

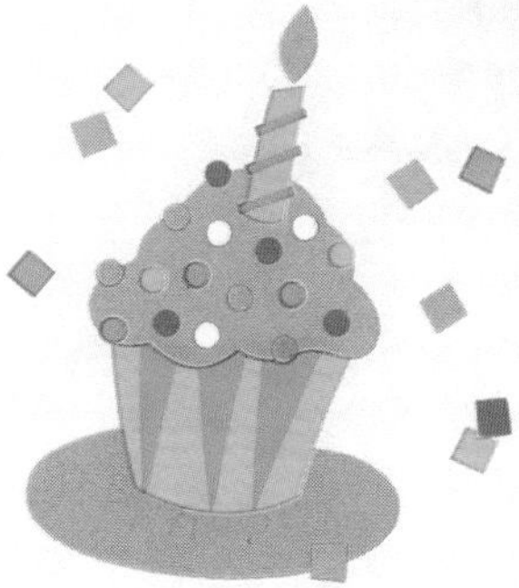

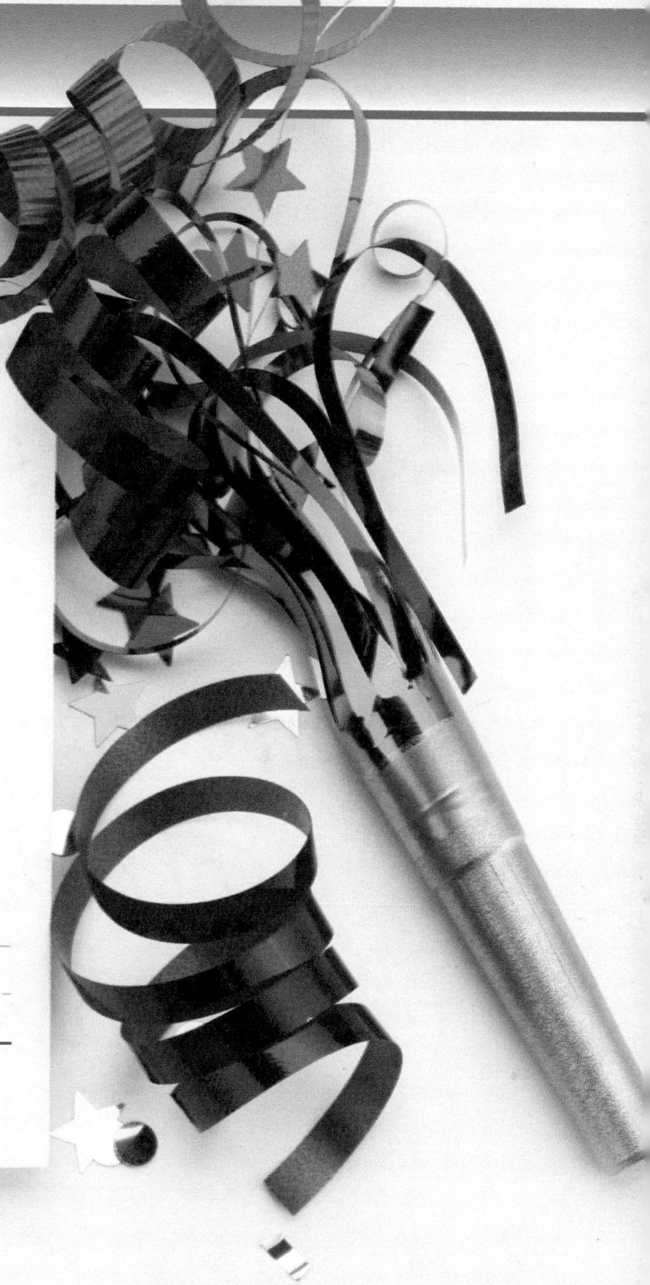

Linking Handwriting to Writing

Writing a Friendly Letter

Read this friendly letter. Look at the three parts.

Dear Marta,
I have good news.
Mom says I can have
a birthday party. We
will have fun.

Kim

This tells who gets the letter.

This tells what you say to your friend.

Your name

Copy the friendly letter from page 118. Write on the lines below.
Do not copy the parts in blue.

ON YOUR OWN Write a letter to a friend. Use your best handwriting.

Writing an Envelope

An envelope needs a name and an address. Look at the envelope below.

The name of the person who gets the letter

Marta Senno

The number of the house and the name of the street

27 Elm Road

The city, the state, and the ZIP code

Austin, TX 78703

▫ **COMPUTER TIP** Computers have keys for typing numbers. Locate the number keys on your computer.

Fill out the envelope below. Use the name and address on page 120.

ON YOUR OWN Write the name and address of someone you might send a letter to, or write your own name and address.

There is no one in the world quite like you. You walk, talk, think, act, and dress in your own special way.

You write in your own special way, too. Look at the size and slant of the words below.

wide   narrow

forward   straight

backward

Use your personal style to write your name.

Copy the title and the first six lines of this poem on your paper.

The Frog on the Log

There once
Was a green
Little frog, frog, frog—

Who played
In the wood
On a log, log, log!

A screech owl
Sitting
In a tree, tree, tree—

Came after
The frog
With a scree, scree, scree!

When the frog
Heard the owl—
In a flash, flash, flash—

He leaped
In the pond
With a splash, splash, splash!

Ilo Orleans

Index